GUIDE TO GET THE GUY

GUIDE TO GET THE GUY

Amador Amado

Copyright © 2024 Amador Amado
All rights reserved.

ISBN: 979-8-9876421-4-6

Thank you, Alicia Cole, for creating the stunning book covers!

There were countless books and stories you could've picked, yet you chose this one for a reason. Just like all the guys out there, you haven't been able to catch the right one yet. So congratulations on your choice. You, as well as many women around the world, are having a hard time picking out the right guy. It's not your fault, so don't blame yourself. There's no need to look in the mirror and ask yourself what is wrong with you either—unless you suffer from psychological issues. If so, you might want to seek professional help. Are you wondering if all the good men are hiding under a rock? They're not; it's just that you weren't taught correctly on what to look for, that's all. Nowadays women are making the same mistakes. Y'all are going for the wrong guy, thinking he's the one. Chances are you're enticed by superficial traits, which won't help in a long-term relationship. Then y'all get too attached right away and place a blindfold over your eyes. You women are theorizing unwisely and creating a dysfunctional market based on others' success. The guy who every other girl is going for might not suit you. There have been many changes in the dating game that you have or have not noticed—chivalry is dead. Most men are checking out with women due to past bad experiences. Women are confused and believe others' secrets will help them, but will they? You seriously believe the chubby, bearded guy is going to make you happy? Is he going to eat your heart out as he scarfs down his next meal? You have trust in the ugly guy that he will not cheat? Or is he just waiting for the next opportunity he didn't have before to have multiple women? You seriously think confiding in that guy who dances great is going to satisfy you? Is he going to dance his way into your life and have the right moves to make it last?

Did you gamble on the tall guy? You seriously believe he's tall enough to reach for the sky and bring you back down a star or two? Or how about the one who has many options to choose from? Did you bet on him picking you out of the pile, or will he just use you without getting to know you properly? Maybe these guys will be great candidates, but there's more to it than you know.

Truth be told, when women seek a mate, they're searching for a father figure. Someone to protect them from harm. Someone to give up his life if need be. A guy who's going to nurture and keep them safe. Does it make sense to you now why you're attracted to tall guys? Literally, someone you look up to and makes you feel little makes you feel safe—like a small kid looking up at her big father and feeling secured from danger. Why do you go crazy for a guy with a strong build? Because you know he looks intimidating enough to keep you out of harm's way. How about a guy with a deep voice? This one is more of an attraction because of your gut instinct and natural self-definition of masculinity. And if you're into bad boys, it makes more sense, doesn't it? You want a guy who's dangerous enough to be respected and feared. Which little girl wouldn't want her father to be described as such? If your father was or is as explained, then why wouldn't you want a man like him? Now that you're feeling hope, don't you go seeking him on your own without finishing this guide. There will be no more excuses for your poor choices. You will learn the differences by the end and will be able to make the best decision of your life all on your own. Well, maybe with a little help from what you'll grasp and recall.

I will agree there are masculine women in search of little boys to mother, but that's not the true nature of a woman in a relationship. That desire is intended for caring after baring your own child, not your partner. These types of women are in search of feminine males to dominate. If this description fits your criteria, you might not want to continue. Most of these gals were brought up in a household in the absence of a male figure. If there was a male model present, he was more than likely a beta or hardly ever there mentally.

They didn't receive the love and support from their fathers to make them know what to look for from their own mothers' experiences. As much as I'd like to cover this topic, it will only divert my intentions, so if you'd like to learn more, search the web where you'll find psychological and physical evidence to back up my point.

Let's get into the lost strategy women failed to pass down through generations. Before life was as we know it now, society worked a bit differently. Just as in the animal kingdom, there was an alpha male. I'm sure you've heard of this terminology before, but it may have not made complete sense. The alpha was self-determined by his own actions unlike nowadays where the alpha is determined by the market y'all established. The alpha male was in charge of the community that he directed and protected. He was predominantly the one all women in the group wanted to mate with in order to secure the best offspring. He was the one who showed little to no fear in battle and the one who had the best genes, generally speaking. Nowadays the alpha male is scarcer than at any other time in history. We now live in a world that exiles the alpha mentality and promotes the beta one. Before you lose the concept of the lesson, I'm going to inform you of the characteristics of an alpha. First of all, the alpha is disciplined in his leadership. He is a warrior, a fighter for what he loves and cares for. He is wise and uses his knowledge for the common good. An alpha male can be pinpointed in a group of guys easily due to his resilience. He sticks out like a sore thumb if you know what to look for. He is usually the one who's discreetly observing things around him, ready to address any issues that may arise—the one who runs toward danger with bravery and not the one who runs from it cowardly. Depending on the situation itself, he is smart enough to avoid problems that don't fuel his purpose. Sounds like the guy you'd like to be with, right?

Here's a checklist to assist you in finding the true alpha masculine characteristics. He must not be feminine, although having feminine features would be a plus for he'll be more attractive. I'm not referring to having man boobs or wide hips with a fat ass either. He should be knowledgeable, and I'm not talking about one who can use his memory or a guide to fix things. I'm talking about wits; can he figure things out on his own? Anyone can be educated, but a sign of good genes is his ability to handle situations by himself. Brains are crucial for life; don't underestimate this very important value. The more manly he is the better. Facial and body hair will lead you on the right path. True warriors had a beard and long hair, which made them less susceptible to being knocked out during combat. You might want to be picky about him having a receding hairline though. Chances are that hairline is a future sign of him losing a battle to baldness. Most men who can grow a full beard end up bald as well, so be cautious. If he's young, look at his ancestors. If they're bald, then chances are he will too one day. Sometimes women are attracted to bald men due to their perception that they look like children, but they're just mixed emotions; he's not a baby. He must have a deep voice. A deep voice proves he's got great masculine genes and high testosterone levels. Make sure he's not faking his voice though; don't be tricked by a performance. You have to remember at some point the alphas from the past had children, and that's what you're looking for—the one with the best qualities. He shall be a fighter, a calculated striker by birth not one who was taught the art of self-defense. A true warrior has it in him for combat, or he learns on his own along the way. There you know he'll fight for you and your offspring. He'll fight for his beliefs and honor—a born leader, not a bossy guy but one who means well with his requests, leading by example and not just manipulating others for his benefit. He should be physically strong as he must be able to handle the weight of the world and the pressure of physical demands. Weakness of either is a dead giveaway; he's not worthy material. He must be loving to be able to put down his sword to embrace you and his children in his loving and caring arms. The ability to manage and regulate his testosterone is beneficial. High testosterone—can you smell the man in him? This chemical can be sensed through your nose. After showering, does he smell masculine? Because all men who do not properly clean can have a masculine odor, so don't be misled. Another indicator of high testosterone is if his left ring finger is longer than his index. He should have a big chest and broad shoulders—a strong physique is a telltale sign you're choosing correctly. Not just strong hands, thick forearms will also direct you. He should also have big biceps and triceps, and not just because he works out but because he was genetically built that way. Is he ambitiously driven by his desire to be free? Going back to brains, his ambition must be rewarding for self-preservation and not driven by women, greed, or evil. Man of his word—he must not procrastinate and should keep his promises. There you'll know his ability to be disciplined. Real men have a bond with their word and don't break it. Has he proved himself to survive adversity? A guy who has been to hell and back has the capability of doing as much good as bad. It also demonstrates he's not a quitter when things go wrong or get rough. Is he respected among his peers, coworkers, and family? If he's respected, then that's a good sign he's disciplined. It shows he has proved himself to not be messed with. With regard to coping with relationships, if he sticks to his guns in disputes, and I don't mean literally, it shows he's firm on his beliefs once again. With respect to getting along with others, the others must approve of him socially, although there are a few who've been through so much they'd rather stick to themselves, so there are exceptions.

If you're asking why all this is important, it matters because if you're planning on having kids, their father's genes serve an important role in their creation and development. Can you picture yourself having children with a guy who has bad looks, is a coward and a deceiver, and is lazy, dumb, and stubborn? Would you really be proud of seeing your child grow up to be just like his daddy? Genes carry down from mothers and fathers. It's not like you could get pregnant from a moron and expect to raise a genius. Even if you're not planning on conceiving a baby from the man you choose, it may happen accidentally or your plans might change. You want your offspring to have the best genes to thrive and survive in this world. You want them to be smart, strong, healthy, and attractive. Picking the last guy on the court to fill the MVP spot could turn out to be catastrophic.

It's been annotated that there are six different types of males. The most commonly known are alphas and betas. The remaining four are gamma, omega, delta, and zeta. I strongly believe in only the first two. You could search the web yourself and read or study the information for your own educational purpose. It's something I'm not going to veer off the lecture at hand to address.

Continuing forward, let's talk about the beta. The beta male is and should be your last option to choose. The reason is that they lack strength both physically and mentally—the total opposite of an alpha. They're weak individuals without the capability genetically speaking of pleasuring a female. They don't have it in them to fight. They don't have it in them to succeed. They don't have it in them to accommodate anyone else other than themselves for their insecurities of knowing the truth. They themselves know they're at the bottom of the barrel of mankind. These peasants have gone unnoticed for centuries as nonthreatening and have developed manipulative ways to trick females along their selfish journey. They're now thriving specimens just as any other endangered species overcoming their own extinction. All this is once again due to the market illogical women have created where they shine decidedly through deception. There are no pros to keeping a beta, who are also known as a simp. There are only cons to doing so. He will never take charge, accountability, or make any right or proper decisions based on common logic. Dealing with personal insecurities of theirs due to their true self will only jeopardize any form of relationship. They are unable to make a woman happy due to their own sad nature, which is one of the most crucial reasons the world is as it is now. The false education women have been taught has led to them expanding and dominating a market, feeding lies to fools, where women are running around with their heads cut off, unable to see the correct direction.

Betas have learned to pretend to be an alpha. After all, they want to get women too. Not only that, but they also gather in groups against the alpha, groups for which they don't even have loyalty and only betray each other. They mimic alpha behaviors to a degree. While some are docile and clearly present themselves as being betas, others hide under their perception of an alpha for their own personal gain to reproduce or dominate. You'd figure this out should you place your thinking cap on correctly. Women need guidance, and if you form a relationship with a beta, he'll guide you all right—to tragedy. A beta's purpose has always been and always will be to attract females. Each and everything they do is for that specific reason. So the loud guy you may view as an alpha nine times out of ten is simply a beta in disgust. That one guy with money and power seducing women more than likely is a beta utilizing his weapons females have crafted for his gain. Just about anything could be learned and remembered in life should it be of any value to one's purpose. After centuries of living side by side, it is ironic to say the thief has continued to make the same mistakes without foreseeing his same strategy will fail once more. And what better way to do so other than observing what the banker does and says—studying each and every deterring action taken or created for the protection of value. This is what betas have been doing with women—learning to deceive them for their personal gain. Y'all have been victimized by a clone of what y'all are really searching for, which is more of a reason to be on guard watching out for small details that otherwise you would have overlooked in the past.

That being said, who exactly do you believe is pursuing you all right now? Definitely not the alpha who has already landed a woman himself, has landed himself a jail sentence for fighting through life in an uneven battle protecting the beta system, or the alpha who's checked out from competing for females because he's too busy focusing on himself. Things are now even easier for the beta to pursue females on social media platforms. An alpha sure isn't going to be competing with multiple guys of no value for a woman allowing a competition in the first place. Only betas themselves are okay with sloppy seconds and leftovers of what at one point they weren't able to have. More than likely, the guys pursuing y'all online are the same ones who wouldn't have the courage to do so in person. So it would be a great idea for you to stop paying attention to those courting you on social media. The thing is as soon as this new tactic is utilized, betas will change and adapt to it. So it's safe to take advantage when the female market changes right before betas catch on.

This is where the problem lies at the moment. Most women have felt an empowerment of value based on being chased by betas. Technology has made human life more comfortable and easier to adapt to the system established in place. These low-quality men have been studying you all under a microscope. They see what you all are searching for and imitate it. They hear women like guys with trucks and they go get one. They hear women like guys with beards and they'll grow one. You females are responsible for the market y'all created. So in order to choose the right guy you must be able to see that one guy you've been talking to should be able to survive without it—capable of outlasting nature in its pure form. (Choose a warrior who will endure apocalyptic events, and stay away from the liars, gossipers, lazy, dumb, procrastinators, and all those low-testosterone feminine men.) Then you'll know you've picked correctly. Always have in mind everything created can be destroyed. You've now been educated on how to choose the right guy, which is only half the battle. Be on the lookout for the following lecture on how to keep him.

I'm thrilled to share with you my previous works, each a piece of my heart and imagination.

I'm excited to announce my upcoming release, "Stale Tales." Stay tuned as I delve into new realms of storytelling, promising to captivate and inspire once again.

Thank you for being part of this incredible journey. Your passion for literature fuels my creativity, and I can't wait to share more adventures with you soon!

www.ingramcontent.com/pod-product-compliance
Lightning Source LLC
Chambersburg PA
CBHW061349040426
42444CB00011B/3162